LET'S TALK ABOUT
BEING LAZY

REVISED FOR EDUCATIONAL USE

By Joy Wilt Berry

Illustrated by John Costanza

CHILDRENS PRESS ®

CHICAGO

Let's talk about BEING LAZY.

Have people ever asked you
to do something for them
that they could have
done for themselves?

5

Has anyone refused
to help you
when you needed help?

7

People who are lazy
sometimes ask others
to do things
they could do themselves.

People who are lazy
sometimes refuse
to help others.

9

When you are with someone who is lazy,

how do you feel?
what do you think?
what do you do?

11

When you are with someone
who is lazy:

You may feel angry and upset.

You may feel it is too much work
to spend time with that person.

You may decide
you'd rather be somewhere else.

It is important to treat others
the way you want to be treated.

If you do not want
those you are with to be lazy,
you must not be lazy.

There are many ways
to keep from being lazy.

You can take care of yourself.

You can clean up after yourself.

You can be helpful.

To take care of yourself,
try not to ask anyone
to do something for you
that you can do for yourself.

17

You can also take care of yourself
by doing these things:

Keep yourself clean.
Take a bath,
wash and comb your own hair,
and brush your own teeth.

Dress yourself.
Decide what clothes
you are going to wear
and put them on yourself

19

To keep from being lazy,
you can clean up after yourself.

Keep your room neat.

Help keep your house neat.
Put things away
after you use them.

Clean up any mess you make.

To keep from being lazy,
you can *be helpful.*

There are many small jobs
you can do:

Set the table for meals.

Clean the table after meals.

Do the dishes.

Empty the trash.

Can you think of other things
you can do to be helpful?

Taking care of yourself,
cleaning up after yourself, and
helping out
may not always be fun.

Sometimes these things are work.

Try to be a good sport
about your work.

Don't complain about it.

Don't wait to be reminded to do it.

Don't try to get out of doing it.

Don't put it off until later.

To make your work more fun,
it might be helpful to do these things:

Play a game with yourself.
Set yourself a time limit and
try to get the job done
in that amount of time.

Reward yourself.
Promise yourself that you will
do something you really want to do
after you finish your job.
Be sure to keep the promise
you make to yourself.

To be happy, treat others
the way you want to be treated.

Everyone is happier
when no one is lazy.

About the Author
Joy Berry is the author of more than 150 self-help books for children. She has advanced degrees and credentials in both education and human development and specializes in working with children from birth to twelve years of age. Joy is the founder of the Institute of Living Skills. She is the mother of a son, Christopher, and a daughter, Lisa.